This Book Belongs to:

_____

_____

_____

-I am a leader.

Welcome To The Universe

A Colorful Introduction to Space.

Written by Maria Moon

Copyright © 2025 by iloveloni
All rights reserved.

No part of this book may be reproduced, stored in a retrieval system, or transmitted in any form or by any means — electronic, mechanical, photocopying, recording, or otherwise — without prior written permission of the publisher, except for brief quotations used in reviews or articles.

For permissions, contact:
iloveloni
books@iloveloni.com
written by Maria Moon

ISBN: 979-8-9932223-4-9
Cover and interior design by iloveloni
Printed in the United States of America

iloveloni

We live on Earth.
Earth is a planet apart of the Universe.

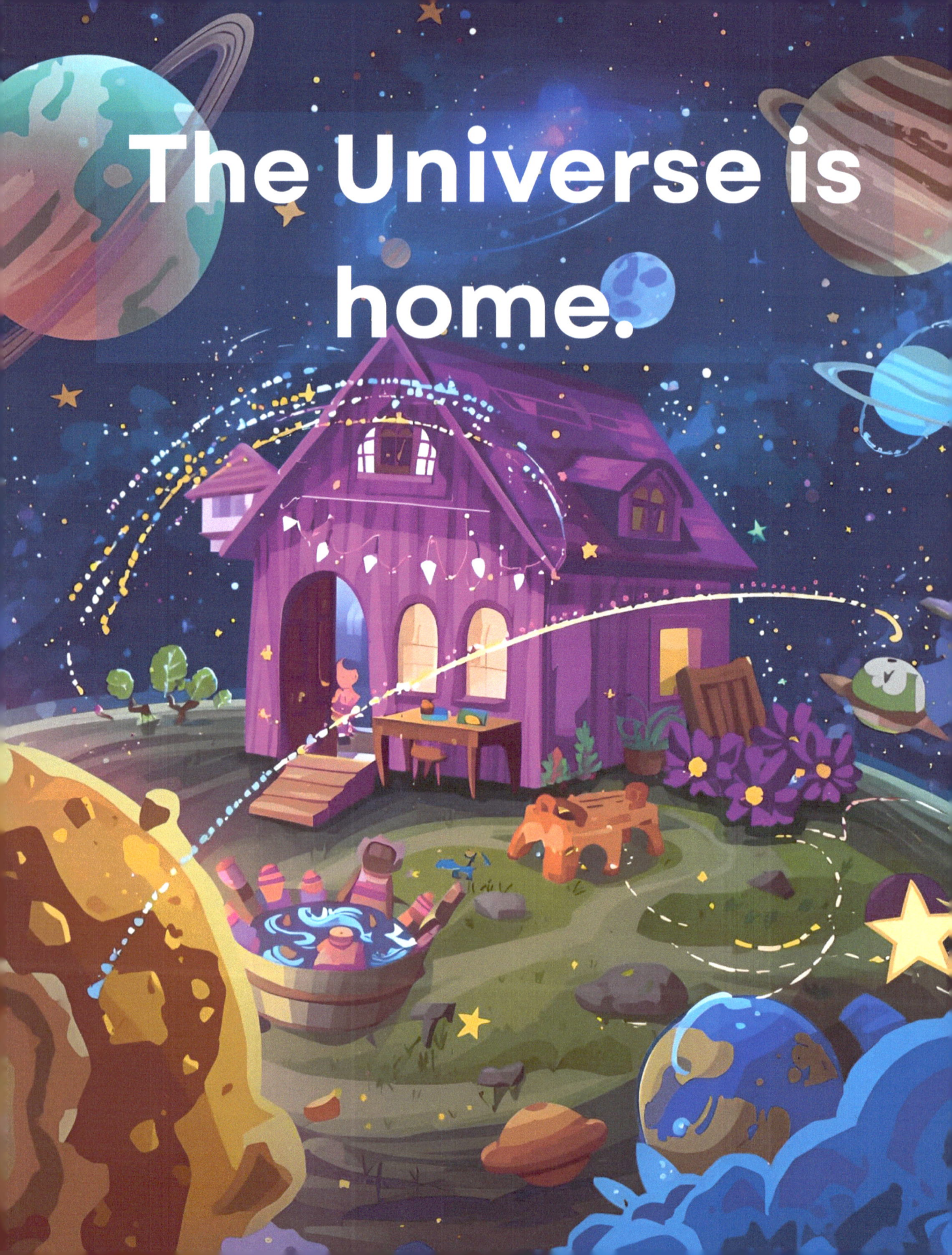

Home to all the stars and planets, Earth is not alone.

All the planets move around the Sun.

The Sun is a ball of hot gas, that gives heat to everyone.

It also controls day and night.

The Sun is a star.
It only seems so big because
the others are so far.

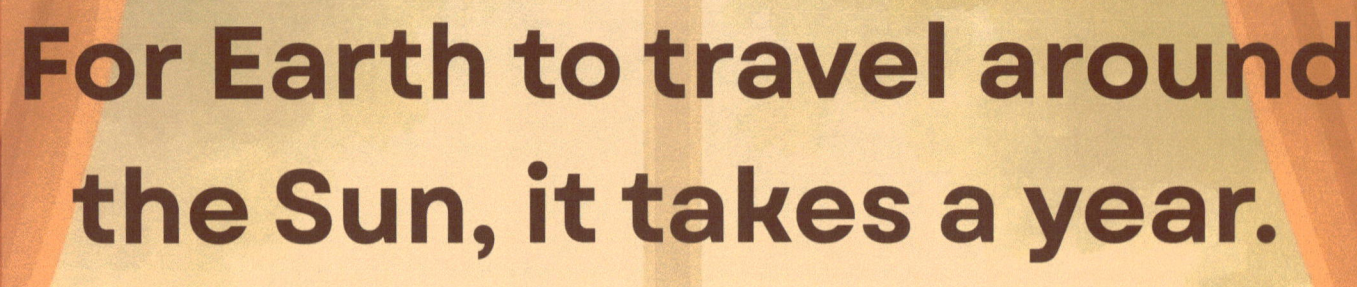

For Earth to travel around the Sun, it takes a year.

The Sun and the Moon control the ocean's flow.

As above, so below.

The Moon stays with us wherever we go.

In the Summer, the Spring, the Fall, and the snow.

The moon also moves on its own.

Its trip around the world takes about a month.

Together their movements make the pattern of time.

The days, months, years and the seasons we live by.

www.ingramcontent.com/pod-product-compliance
Lightning Source LLC
Chambersburg PA
CBHW061158030426
42337CB00003B/48